MW00424419

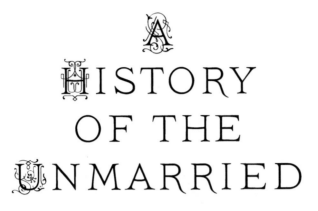

A HISTORY OF THE UNMARRIED

Stephen S. Mills

SIBLING RIVALRY PRESS
LITTLE ROCK, ARKANSAS
WWW.SIBLINGRIVALRYPRESS.COM

A History of the Unmarried
Copyright © 2014 by Stephen S. Mills

Cover photo copyright © OurFamilyAlbum.org
Used with permission
Author photo courtesy Stephen S. Mills
Cover design by Mona Z. Kraculdy

Sibling Rivalry Press, LLC
PO Box 26147
Little Rock, AR 72221
info@siblingrivalrypress.com

www.siblingrivalrypress.com

ISBN: 978-1-937420-79-6

Library of Congress Control Number: 2014944839

First Sibling Rivalry Press Edition, September 2014

For My Mother

*"Now I'm quietly waiting for
the catastrophe of my personality
to seem beautiful again,
and interesting, and modern."*

— Frank O'Hara

A HISTORY OF MARRIAGE

I.

My parents married in October, 1973.
Fall in Indiana. The smell of burning
leaves. Browns. Oranges. Reds.
The world shrinking down, preparing
for winter—dying. 1973. The same year
Richard Nixon said, *I'm not a crook*
to a crowd in Orlando, Florida,
and the American Psychiatric
Association removed homosexuality
from its list of mental disorders.
The same year of *Roe vs. Wade*
and the opening of the World Trade
Center. A year of change. In October,
my mother stood in a wedding dress
white as Indiana winters. My father
in a tuxedo beside her. Friends
and family gathered. A minister
presided. Vows were taken. It was
a wedding that set into motion a life.
A family. A bond of two bodies.
One man. One woman. It was the same
year Jackson Pollock's *Blue Poles* sold
for two million dollars, and a gas shortage
closed stations on Sundays leaving
everyone desperate for a full tank.
It was October, 1973. Leaves
on the ground. Fall in Indiana.

II.

There were days when we mimicked
them. When you got down on one
knee, a ring in hand. When *yes I said*
yes I will Yes. When we bought
wedding magazines, made guest lists,
thought of color combinations.
There were days when our Midwest
upbringing made a wedding, legally
recognized or not, seem to matter most.
There were days when you felt like
a husband. Like my father. Like
a shadow of a life I was meant to have.

III.

Brides magazine says June is the month
to marry. Sunshine. Flowers in bloom.
The world exploding with new life.
A new start. My sister married in June,
1997. I was 14. She was 19. A young
bride like my mother. Again in Indiana.
1997. The year Timothy McVeigh
was convicted of murder in the Oklahoma
City bombing and Princess Diana died
in that car crash. Our faces gathered
in TV light crying for a woman we didn't
know. A princess that wasn't ours to have.
Sylvia Plath also married in June.
June of 1956. She'd only known Ted
Hughes a few short months.
She was in awe of him, his poetry,
his drive, but that didn't end so well,
did it? 1956. The same year Jackson
Pollock drove drunk and crashed his car,

killing him and his current fling—not
his wife. My sister never read Plath
or Hughes. Never stood before a Pollock.

IV.

There were days when we hated them.
When we despised the wedding
invitations in the mailbox, the gift
registries, the bachelorette parties
at the gay club: the girls bouncing
up and down with pink plastic penises
on their heads, which made us wonder
if they'd ever seen a real one.
There were days when we felt evolved.
Our couple-hood our own.
No wedding required. No paperwork.
No public announcement. Then there
was the day I slipped my ring off
my left hand and onto my right.
Our symbol. Our sign. Not theirs.

V.

Grace Kelly married the Prince
of Monaco in 1956. She never acted
again, but is best known for her roles
in Hitchcock's *Dial M for Murder*
and *Rear Window*. She died in a car
crash the same year I was born.
1982. The year William Bonin
was convicted of being a Freeway
Killer. One of three. He admitted
to killing and raping 21 young men
and dumping them beside the California
freeway. Sometimes with the help

of his friend Vern. He became the first
person in California put to death
by lethal injection. People say January
Jones, who plays Betty Draper on *Mad
Men*, looks a lot like Grace Kelly.
Beautiful. Blonde. Betty marries Don.
A picture perfect couple. Spoiler Alert:
it doesn't last. Raymond Burr,
another 1950's actor, who played Perry
Mason, had two fake marriages
and then a real one, which he annulled
a few months later. The time of year
doesn't seem to matter in that case.
Summer? Fall? The dead of winter?
Later he met a man. They grew orchids
together. Fell in love. Grew old.

VI.

There were days when we spoke
of leaving. Of moving to Canada,
Spain, South Africa. The poster boys
of marriage equality. There were days
we felt defeated by our own desires.
Our bodies moving in different
directions. There were days we
accepted the beauty of our love.
Our choices. Our rules. There were
days spent with other men. Nights
in other bodies. Sometimes together.
Sometimes alone. There was the day
we separated love and sex and placed
them in boxes beside the bed. No longer
needing approval. There were fights
in the bright sunlight of our apartment
and in the shadows of night

where fights are meant to thrive
and eventually die. Then there were days
when we could only bear each other.
My body on your body. The world
outside desperate to define us.

STANDING IN FRONT OF POLLOCK'S
SUMMERTIME: NUMBER 9A, LONDON, 2003

I like to imagine I saw you coming.
          Had some premonition
as I stood alone before Pollock:
          fresh out of the closet,
                    just twenty,
and in Europe for the first time.

Spring and British boys
          everywhere.
Boys who confused me
          with their neck scarves
                    and ambiguous
                              sexuality.

You were coming for me just after
          the summertime,
at the beginning of fall,
          back home
                    in Indiana.
My London adventures
          behind me.
Your college adventures
          just beginning.

That May I spent hours in the Tate,
          in front of Jackson's long,
                              skinny painting
(the first I ever saw of his).
          Spent hours watching
                    for other gay boys.
Gay men.

Men I'd follow around
           and around.
        Making up my own game:
If he comes back to the Pollock,
      I'll say hello, I'll tap my foot,
I'll bump into him,
      I'll make all the faces
I've practiced from watching too many
      episodes of Queer *as* Folk:
           my gay manual.
I'll make him fall in love with me,
      right here in front of paint splatters.
           I'll stay in London.
I'll never go back.
      Never.

But at the end of the day,
      it was always me
           and Pollock.
The museum about to close.
      Summertime coming fast.
         Then fall.
Then you.

NOT MY MOTHER ,

My mother never drank gin
or smoked cigarettes.
She never had fine dresses:
perfectly detailed, beaded,
elegant. She never turned
heads with her model grace:
icy, but beautiful.
No one ever called her
a dead ringer for Grace
Kelly. My mother never
smacked me across
the face in a sudden,
unexpected fury,
though I deserved it
a time or two.
Like when I poured
garlic salt all over
the living room carpet
as if some superstitious
Italian grandmother
had overtaken my still-
growing body, or the time
I called 911, age 5,
just to chat. The police
arriving quickly,
startling my mother
working in the front yard.
No, my mother never
slapped me in a dramatic
tense-filled scene. Tears
streaming down my face.

She never stared into
the distance as if
the whole world might
suddenly crack open
just beyond the tip
of her cigarette.
She never modeled fur
coats. Never owned one.
Not even a fake
like the one I bought
to smear red paint on
as a Halloween costume
a few years ago. She was never
the almost-face of Coca-Cola.
Never married
a dark handsome man
with a troubled past
and a weakness for anything
in a skirt. Instead she married
a good, solid Midwestern man.
A man who came home
on time. Never drank.
Never cheated. Never hid
behind another identity
like I did for twenty years.
No, my mother never shot
the neighbor's pigeons,
standing in her nightgown
with cigarette and shotgun.
Though I wish she had.

HOUSEWIFE ETIQUETTE: RULE I

To be a good wife, prepare yourself before he comes home from work. Fifteen minutes before, refresh yourself. Touch up your make-up. Put a ribbon in your hair. He's spent the day with a lot of work-weary people. He wants something nice to look at when he comes home. He deserves it. Be gay and interested.

Mistaken Identity

When I type your name into Google
my screen fills with links to a Dustin
Carter I don't know: a young man
who's a state champion high school
wrestler from Ohio, who had all four
of his limbs amputated when he was 5.
When I click "images," as anyone
would, there he is in full color: a body
trimmed away, yet still he dominates
the mat. His half-arms, half-legs stretching
in every direction, pinning down
the other boys with his 103 pounds
of power and spandex, not unlike you
pinning me to the bed—naked.
I wonder if some day you'll be mistaken
for this boy. Perhaps at an airport.
Say the ticket agent sees your name
and he's from Ohio, played basketball,
but was always overshadowed by a limbless
wrestler who got a story in *Sports Illustrated*.
This agent seeks revenge and just
as he's about to give you a seat between
two annoying passengers with screaming
children he'll look up, see your limbs intact,
realize his mistake, but disappointment
will make him give you the seat anyway,
because for a second you and Wrestler
Carter will have been the same person.

Like someday I might be mistaken
for the Judo blogger who shares my name
and enjoys expressing his love of martial
arts to strangers. I read his posts,

though I don't even know what Judo is
exactly, but I imagine it can be quite thrilling
for those who appreciate the way bodies
move in space: the visual representation
of violence. Blogger Mills ends each post
with the words: "keep smiling" and I wonder
what he has to smile about. Judo? His ability
to look good in white? Or maybe the new
sexual positions he's created based on
this ancient art of moving? He addresses
his readers as if there are hundreds,
maybe thousands, yet no one has left
a comment, making me think his audience
is actually quite small, might only be made up
of other Stephen Millses who found his blog
by narcissistically searching Google
for their own reflection—which I find
when I switch my search to "images" (safe
filter off). It's a picture with both a Dustin
Carter and a Stephen Mills, and it's really us.
We're standing in suits about to kiss, flowers
in our lapels. It's from the mock weddings
we did in college to help show the Midwest
that gay people aren't so scary, but the local
newspaper refused to publish a photo
of two young men about to kiss at a fake
wedding, so the photographer posted it
on his webpage instead. There we are
in cyberspace: two boys in love. And I wonder
if that wrestler or blogger has ever typed
his name into Google, hit "images," and stared
in amazement at us, thinking: *Maybe one day
I'll be mistaken for a boy who kissed another boy
on a cold February day in Indiana.*

You Don't Kiss Boys, Boys Kiss You

But what if you are a boy?
What then, Betty Draper?
What does your manners
book say? What's the dating
etiquette for us queers?
Don't look so shocked.
Like you don't sense it.
The men who look at you
in awe that has nothing
to do with sexual desire.
They aren't imagining
your breasts that fit
so perfectly in your dress
and cardigan. They don't
imagine taking you to bed
or undoing your undergarments,
which I'm sure are more
complicated than any math
problem ever set before you.
You've seen them. The men
who worship you for your beauty.
For your coldness. For the way
you slap your daughter
in the face. What are the rules
for kissing boys when you
are, in fact, a boy yourself?
Betty, help us. We'll love you
longer and harder than
any straight man.

REAL MEN LOVE JESUS

Four years ago a little boy on the streets of Madison,
        Indiana yelled at us, *It's Adam and Eve,*
not Adam and Steve, and I wanted to tell him
        my name was in fact Stephen, Steve, if he wanted.
Though I never let anyone call me that
        except for my French professor in college,
who terrified me and thought if he spoke French louder
        I would eventually understand. I never did.
Of course your name isn't Adam,
        so the point would've been moot,
and the boy would've still hated us—but loved Jesus.

        Like your grandfather who was a pastor, not formally
trained, one of those backwoods Southern Indiana pastors
        with fire in their bellies and a Bible in their hands.
You tell me he cursed like a sailor,
        but somehow that fits my image of the righteous,
of those who think being born once isn't good enough,
        and maybe it's not. Or of those who litter
college campuses with indestructible "tickets to heaven."

        And I'm reminded of the lesbian in my poetry workshop
who found one in the restroom and spent the entire class
        struggling to rip the ticket in two
as if she thought this would mean God doesn't exist
        and these crusaders truly are fools.
But foolishness is in the eye of the beholder, I thought
        as I watched her struggle, cursing at the plastic,
probably made by the government in a secret lab
        far beneath the earth's surface
where it feels a lot like hell, sort of like it does in Florida

where last week two Baptist boys approached us
in the parking lot of the Super Target wanting to invite us
        to their church. We simply said, *We're gay*
and off they went—fast across the asphalt,
        looking back only once to confirm
they had actually met two faggots buying shaving cream
        and toilet paper. I imagine them meeting up
with their buddies saying, *They look just like us!*
        We've got to be more careful. Maybe next time
they'll wear rubber gloves, face masks, have their gaydar gun
        ready as they scan the parking lot,
searching for real men.

WE'VE DONE THIS ALL BACKWARDS

and now attempt to fix it with bodies
that might satisfy the urges in our guts
that say love came too quick, too fast.

But we know they will fade: the men
we will fuck, like the porn we once
so carefully downloaded and burned

to discs that now sit unused beneath
old photographs you took of me:
my body as white as clouds moving

across your black backdrop. What was it?
A table cloth? A sheet? The cover
to your old futon which you bought

for 20 bucks from some frat boy in college?
Somehow we've forgotten the details.
We make rules for our game of hook-up:

condoms always, full disclosure.
Part of me thinks you want this
for the good stories I'll tell.

How I'll weave tales of bubble-butted
boys with silly screen-names and bodies
that never live up to their digital avatars.

Tonight, I give it a try. You away
on business, me trolling the Internet
for boys, or are they men?

One man wants pissed on, another told
stories of childhood spankings as he jerks
off in the corner. Not sure what's in it for me.

It's hard being an adventurous sex maniac
on the prowl at 3 AM, our bed empty,
the dog licking his ass. Tomorrow, you'll come

home with bags, a kiss hello, and questions
in your throat: *Did I? Did he? Was it?*
Though we both know none of it matters.

None of it will erase my hand touching yours
all those years ago, or how my body, that first time,
slipped into yours and nearly vanished.

SEEING A DEAD LIZARD AFTER READING MARK DOTY'S "TURTLE, SWAN"

His body is crushed above his front
legs. His head cocked forward and up.
One eye bugging out of socket. From
a few feet away he still looks alive
as if he might scurry into the bushes

at any moment. But he doesn't move.
The other lizards take no notice:
still swim across the grass, their legs
paddling against the uneven blades
as I enter the courtyard, my dog in tow.

Even he won't go near the lizard.
Doesn't want to sniff it, has no
intention of putting it in his mouth,
for he is particular (or is it distrusting?)
of what he closes his mouth around.

If only I was as cautious. By the next
morning the lizard is gone. Picked up
by the yardmen? Maybe. Carried off
and buried by the kids who live below
us? A lesson in death? Probably not.

Those kids are more likely to set fire
to the building than to care for
the body of a dead lizard. Maybe
he's still there in the cement, melted
down by the hot Florida sun, not even

leaving a stain—no remains. At night
in our bed, the story of the lizard
two flights down, I make you promise
I won't die alone, like the gay couple
we read about who didn't get to say

goodbye, didn't have the right paperwork,
weren't a family. The one in the back
of the ambulance dying of a heart attack.
The other forced to follow in his car
whispering: *Don't let him die, don't let him die.*

But he did. We don't have paperwork,
the right kind or the wrong kind. No
legal document ties my body to yours.
Some days I allow myself to think
of losing you, of you suddenly gone.

As a young boy, I read those books
of strange disappearances, like the farmer
who walked into his cornfield
and never came out. *Vanished*, they say,
which is fitting for two boys

who escaped the corn-soaked land
of Indiana, where we once ventured
into an old movie theater to watch
Vincent Price in *House of Wax* (the 3-D
version). The red velvet of the seats

worn thin, springs creaking with each
movement, each readjustment. There
in the dark, straight Midwestern
couples all around, you took my hand,
whispered how beautiful I was, leaned

your head into mine. Our cardboard
glasses touched, bent, my eyes
blurred, then re-focused and suddenly
everything came to life: bounced off
the screen, off our faces, out of our seats.

Election Night, November 2008

"It's the answer spoken by young and old, rich and poor, Democrat and Republican, black, white, Latino, Asian, Native American, gay, straight, disabled and not disabled— Americans who sent a message to the world that we have never been a collection of Red States and Blue States: we are, and always will be, the United States of America,"

— *President Obama*

I've never been patriotic. Not even when I was selected
        as the flag boy in fifth grade, raising and lowering
the stars and stripes each day, then returning them
        to the principal's filing cabinet. The same principal
who later gave me the citizenship award for being the model
        student. The boy with potential. Another way
to mark me as different, as if the boys who bullied
        weren't doing a good enough job.

And I hate the 4th of July. All those fireworks remind me
        of being here in Florida when I was eleven.
The wind from the stormy day blowing debris
        onto my head with each chandelier of light slinking
down the sky. The beach littered with burning shells, sparks,
        and ash. The hotel rattling with each violent burst
like a war zone. Only the drunk remained: dancing,
        swinging bottles, singing the national anthem.

Later that same night, a drunk patriot got hit by a car
        in the tourist-filled streets of St. Pete Beach,
and my mother, a newly-minted nurse, went to her,
        saw her bleeding body, did what all her years
of studying told her to do, and I think the woman lived
        because the drunk lack alarm, lack the knowledge
of how much easier it is to succumb
        to the warmth of July pavement.

Then there were the fireworks in Kentucky the year
　　　we first fell in love, you and I; a little black
girl, maybe eight, harassed us on the way out, called us *fags,*
　　　and we could do nothing—absolutely nothing,
because even a redneck-Kentucky crowd will side
　　　with a little black girl over two queers.
It's important to know the hierarchy of hate.

No, I've never felt patriotic, not when the Governor
　　　of New Jersey got outed and went on TV
declaring, *I'm a gay American.* Actually, I felt cheated—
　　　and even tonight, when the world is full
of change and this man, who I want to believe in,
　　　says the word *gay* on TV, acknowledging
I exist, I still don't feel it. I turn to you, my lover—
　　　my best friend—and know with our newly-elected
president of hope, we are still alone.
　　　Like little boys in an auditorium in Indiana
being called good citizens, when everyone knows
　　　it's better to be the class clown.

A Stranger Asks:
Who's the Man and Who's the Woman?

She wants to know how to see us.
How to build our boxes. How to paint
our portraits, our diagrams, our insides
spilled on mattresses wet with bodily
fluids. She wants to put us back
together again. Place Part A into Part B.
She wants to know if I don a party dress
and you a tuxedo. If I scrub the toilet
and you change the oil in the car.
She wants to know if we were "normal,"
who would carry the children? Who
would pack the lunches? Sew the Halloween
costumes? Punish the little brats
with a wooden paddle? She wants to know
whose body part goes where. How to
connect our dots. Wants the answer
to the equation: one man + one man =
She's bad at math. Needs a tutor.
What if Part A goes into Part B
and sometimes C and vice versa?
She doesn't understand.

Not Telling My Parents I'm in Therapy While Driving Over the Sunshine Skyway Bridge, Which Collapsed 31 Years Ago

My mother reads the history of the bridge to us
on her new smart phone: [*It's popular with jumpers,
and a common place to shoot car commercials.
An estimated 130 people have jumped off the bridge.*]
My father isn't listening very closely
and the car is drifting toward the center line
as he peers out across the bay. His driving
gets worse each time I see him. My mother
continues, *In response to so many suicides, the state
of Florida installed six crisis telephones along the bridge.*
I guess this means we're responsible for getting
help, if a suspected jumper is spotted. But what
does one look like? My boyfriend, sitting next
to me, wonders aloud, *What height does water
become like concrete?* He's read it somewhere,
but none of us know. It's strange to think
of water as hard and imposing as concrete.
This bridge is a piece of my childhood,
which my mother won't find written in her
Wikipedia entry. My parents drove us over
this bridge each summer while on vacation
in St. Pete Beach. For a family born and raised
in landlocked Indiana, the sight of water
and the need for such a bridge amazed
and astonished us all. But today, even as
my mother reads that The Travel Channel
named this bridge number three in the world,
it doesn't seem nearly as impressive as it once did.
What does? I'm nearing the end of my 20s
and now live just an hour and a half

from this bridge, which collapsed, killing 40
people, in 1980. Two years before I was born.
My parents argue in the front seat if that date
is correct: *I didn't think it was that long ago.*
But time passes quickly. My mother is now
reading about the Summit Venture disaster.
It's named after the ship that hit the bridge
support causing ten cars and a Greyhound bus
to plummet into the Tampa Bay. It was May.
7:30 AM. Storming. It was an accident.
No drunk captain. No pirates. No terrorists.
Just life and death at its most random.
The cars and bus fell 150 feet. Only one man
survived. His car fell onto the deck of the ship.
This random act of chance saved his life.
But old Wesley couldn't get over the fact
that he was the only survivor. See, even random
miracles aren't enough to save us from our own
insanity. Neither is money. The ship company
awarded him a $175,000 settlement, but he spent
the last nine years of his life haunted by falling
cars, collapsing concrete, the smell of saltwater.
My father and boyfriend are laughing as we near
the end of the bridge. My mother has moved on
to reading about some daredevils who tried
to bungee jump off the bridge in '97, but instead
plunged 60 feet into the water. It was all caught
on tape and aired on the TV show *Destroyed in Seconds.*
Now we are back on solid ground. My boyfriend
has reached over and grabbed my hand. My father
is searching for a place to make a U-turn,
so we can go back across the bridge. The trip over
is all we came for: the satisfaction of reliving
my childhood. That's when a bird comes out
of nowhere and by chance death is sliding down
the windshield in the form of limp wings, feathers,

and beak. Startled, we catch our breaths and talk
at once. No one saw it coming, but we all heard
the thud and then the silence. The bird gone.
Our windshield not even cracked. We make
our U-turn, head back toward the bright yellow
cables of the Sunshine Skyway Bridge. My mother
has put away her phone and is trying to change
the subject. But my mind returns to Wesley
and the nightmare he must have had each night
of those nine years. The one of him just missing
the ship deck and plunging into the water.
His car slowly sinking. His hands frantic
on the door handle, the window crank, the back
glass. Unable to do anything. His eyes glued
to the sinking cars all around him and to the bus
coming faster and faster toward the ocean floor.
The passengers' eyes dulling, but never closing.
Wesley beginning to fade himself and then suddenly
waking in a cold sweat. Alive. A wife beside him.
A bird chirping at his open window.

Watching *Sylvia* While You Cart the Dying

Daniel Craig is hotter than Ted Hughes.
Notice, they don't let you get a good glimpse
of his abs, which are obviously defined.
His back and brief nipple shot proves
he is no Hughes, but it's more believable
this way. Sexier too. Paltrow is not a bad
Plath. I buy it. She plays smart white woman
in pain pretty well. Her hair the perfect
shade of blonde. She also played the lead
in the *Dial M for Murder* remake in the 90s:
A Perfect Murder. That time she was the cheater,
but still the good guy. Funny how that works.

You got held over at work again. Another
patient to transport to hospice. Maybe
another old woman who can't remember
where she is or where she's been and hates
you for taking her to a new place she won't
remember. Hates you for strapping her
to a gurney, for talking softly in her ear.
She'll call you a *cunt* as you wheel her down
halls full of women she can't remember.
Their faces sliding by in a blur. These women
have lived longer than they should've. Medical
advancements prolonging the inevitable.

And here I am at home watching a woman
die before her time, just thirty years old.
I know what comes next: Hughes's eyes will
grow more tired. Plath will grow more paranoid.
She'll write better poems. And you, a few miles
away, will look actual death in the face.
Old or young? I don't know. Like the 30-year-old

cancer patient you had last week. She's probably
dead now. Gone. You know I hate the stories
you tell at night when I can smell the death
clinging in the thick fibers of your uniform.
But let's not think of that now.

As a teenager, I convinced myself I loved
Gwyneth Paltrow. In my gay mind, she was
a good choice when guys started talking
of celebrity crushes, but I forgot straight boys
love big tits. She's not very sexy as Plath.
Most straight boys would run, but Craig is hot
spouting poetry and cheating his way
through life. Things are falling apart.
Hughes is leaving. Plath is cracking.
You are still gone. Someday this could be us.
The splitting apart. The shouts. The cries.
We've had them, but we've always stayed.

No one has sealed the dog in the bedroom
and done the oven thing. The movie doesn't
show much of her death, but we see her
carried out draped in a bright red blanket,
snow all around. It's winter now, but we're
in Florida where there's no snow and it's nearly
80 degrees. It is here that you handle the dying.
The people left behind. Plath is dead. Hughes
is crying. The credits are rolling. You'll be home
soon, and I'll be naked in bed. Gin on my breath.
The dog curled at my feet. The TV turned off.
Everyone alive for another day.

HOUSEWIFE ETIQUETTE: RULE 9

Minimize all noise. Make sure the dishwasher, washing machine, dryer, and vacuum are all off. He's been in a noisy office all day and wants some peace and quiet. You want all household chores clearly completed before he walks in the door. This is your job, and you want to appear quite good at it. Make sure the children are quietly playing when he arrives. Coming home to noisy children can be quite off-putting.

COUNTING BEARS

You want to go camping. To feel the hardness
of the ground. The rustle of leaves and twigs
beneath you. You want to start a fire. Roast
marshmallows. Tell ghost stories. Something
we've never done together. In fact, you've never
camped with or without me. I, on the other hand,
was a Cub Scout. I've spent nights in tents. Days
fishing. I've built fires. Gathered wood. I've earned
patches, learned the mating calls of birds,
and how to spot poison ivy. Of course, I never
came close to danger. You and I did spend
that weekend in the woods with gay bears,
but I don't think that counts, and we had a cabin
anyway. That was the year you got Hepatitis A.
Your eyes turned yellow. Your skin too,
which seemed so beyond modern day. Your body
suddenly overcome with disease as if it was the 19th
century and you were on your deathbed.
I your nurse. On that weekend, you were a bit
better, but still couldn't drink, which didn't stop me.
After all, it was bear weekend at a clothing-optional
gay campground, and I'm a redheaded twink,
aka Bear Food. There I counted bears. The 59th
was the silver daddy who carried my naked ass
around the pool as I tugged repeatedly on the silver
rings jabbed through each of his hairy nipples.
He was a gentle soul. Soft spoken. Polite.

Our first vacation together was to Vegas
where we took a day trip to see the Grand Canyon.
To be one with nature, but still we didn't camp.
I was just 21. You 19. How small we were.
How insignificant in the face of grandeur.

You wanted to do the horseback trip down
into the canyon, but you're allergic to horses
and wouldn't have made it out alive. Some things
are worth dying for, I suppose, but which things?
Camping? It's full of danger. Wild beasts. Dying
trees that randomly fall and crush you to pieces
in your sleep. Forest fires. Bear attacks. Bad
sense of direction and terrible map skills.
But hotels aren't much safer. There was
that time in Louisville that we jumped awake
to the fire alarm blaring and firemen running
up the stairs. We were on the 16th floor. Terrified.
It was just a false alarm, but still tragedy seemed
only a bed away. We've never been good at preparing
for disaster. Six years in Florida and still no
emergency hurricane kit. No extra water.
No canned food. Just us. At the gay campground,
we were also startled awake, that time by a bear
pounding his fist on our door, howling like a wild
beast that he'd lost his clothes somewhere.
Was it in our cabin? *No.* Naked and drunk, he stood
on the porch for what felt like hours as we huddled
together in bed unwilling to unlatch the door
and let him in. *Never invite a bear to a picnic.* We breathed
a sigh of relief when he stumbled down the steps
and off into the woods to find other bears, other cabins,
maybe even his clothes hanging in a tree. By then
I'd lost count. I saw only you: yellow and beautiful.

Shut Up, Betty! You're Drunk!

I.

He's looking at her   me   from across the car.
There's gin on our breath.   Hers.   Mine.
He's disgusted   by her   me.

I want the window   rolled down.   Fresh air.
She pouts.   He yells.   I pound
a fist   into the glove box.   Throbbing pain.

Nothing.   He says   *shut up*.
We're drunk.   Her.   Me.
Streetlights streak   blonde hair   red hair.

She coils away.   No seatbelt.   I'm stuck.
Belt on stomach   chest   shoulder.
Trapped.   Suffocating.   Bound

by plastic   and steel.   By the thought
of her   me.   A body
curling back   into itself.   Fetal.

Scared.   Drunk?   *Yes*.
But more.   Much   more.
She's there   in the car.   I'm there.

He's there.   The drama   lost
on no one.   To feel   real.
A couple.   A fight.   She's gone

I've gone   we've gone   too far.

II.

She wakes   I wake   with pounding head.
Heads.   We rub eyes   searching
searching   for the man   in our bed.

There'll be   soft sorrys   tears
regrets   promises made   clichés.
He will   forgive.   He won't

forget.   Nor can she.   Nor I.
When he's gone   she will   I will
stand   before the mirror searching

searching   eyes   hers
mine   for the girl   for the boy
for anyone   who once   inhabited them.

III.

I understand
could slap
of a busy

for physical touch.
the suddenness
Mine.

Hands on face.
I am handsome.
the desire

Present.
I understand
I become

mislabeled
how she moves
with such grace.

in a moment.
I understand
I understand

how she
another person
grocery store.

Skin to skin.
of emotions.
How they become

She is beautiful.
Put together.
for contact.

To be heard.
how quickly
we become

misread.
how I move
Grace

Skin on skin.
our hands
her

how I
in the middle
The need

I understand
Hers.
actions.

Elegant.
I understand
To be noticed.

A voice.
she becomes
misunderstood

I understand
how we move
that shatters

Gone.
moving in space.
me.

IV.

She's on the screen glowing. I'm in front
of the screen watching. He's beside
me. In front of her.

I stare at her beauty. At her strange
childlike expressions. Her inability
to accept her life my life.

I'm her. She's me. Both disappointed
in the reality of growing up of men
of life. She did I did

we did what was expected. She pours
a drink. I follow her lead.
I know when she snaps. When she cries.

When she lights another cigarette. I know
how it ends. Where she's going.
She's stuck. I'm stuck. We're stuck.

He flips off the TV.

Holding Hands Outside a Pro-Family Rally with My Seed Inside You

Seed that won't ever take root.
Or grow into a sapling: a start
to a life that may or may not
be worth living. Not all seeds
are meant for the long haul.
Some die young, ripped from
the soil too soon. Some never
stand a chance, like mine
somewhere up inside you
where you like to keep it as long
as possible. The people inside
are talking about family, about
values, about saving marriage.
They come and go from the doors,
faces pale and confused
by the crowd that has gathered
peacefully with signs about love,
equality, acceptance. They firmly
believe in our sinfulness, in our
wrongdoing, yet I doubt most
of them can even imagine
the things we've done,
which might warrant such
judgments. I also doubt that any
of them are thinking about
the possibility of my seed inside
you at this very moment. Doubt
they know how long you can hold it
within you, or how long you can still
feel my cock hours after we've fucked.
I doubt they would call this love,

though I can't think of any other way
to define it as I stand here
with my hand in your hand knowing
pieces of me are still inside you—
still desperate to survive.

Seven Years and Still No Birthday Gift from Your Parents

It's not that I'm greedy. I got over having mountains of gifts
        at a young age, back in Indiana, when my birthday
was celebrated alongside Thanksgiving, sometimes falling
        on the exact same day. Thankfully, I love pumpkin pie.

It's not about money, or the odd gift I might receive
        (What do you purchase for the man who fucks
your son, a man you've only spoken to five times in seven
        years?). And it's not about how funny the birthday

card would be or wouldn't be. Instead, it's about your mother
        writing my name, addressing me directly, at the same
address as you. It's cold in Indiana and still 80 degrees here
        in Florida. I imagine your parents huddled around

their antique fireplace, your mother inking my name,
        then questioning your father on how to close it:
Sincerely? Love? To my son's lover? My son's roommate?
        To the boy who broke our hearts, stole our child?

So many options. Perhaps this is why it never gets in the mail,
        never handed to me by a mailman, sweaty and bent
on transferring north, where there are seasons. It's been seven
        years. Like seven years of bad luck, or the seven deadly

sins, or just the one. Yes, seven years of you and me. Not a phase.
        Not a momentary lapse of judgment.
There's no girl that will suddenly appear on their doorstep,
        like I did that day in December, nearly seven years ago,

when I drove to your parents' house for the first time to take you
    home with me, to save you from their wrath,
from your mother's tears, from them forbidding you to see me.
    How I came while they were at work and we snuck out,

packed what we could into bags that fit in the back of my car.
    How I held your hand all the way to my parents'
house, a two hour drive through the snowy back roads
    of the Midwest, where deer leap in front of cars

and where I was a hero. You my damsel in distress. Your parents
    the villain. My old Buick our white stallion.

On Becoming Domestic Partners, Orlando, 2012

I take you to be my domestic partner. May we live domestically ever after. Isn't that domestic? Oh yes, my domestic partner is so domestically domestic. Cute and domestic, domestically speaking. My domestic partner has the cutest domestic ass. So domestic when he sways around our domestic home doing his domestic chores in the most regularly domestic way. I heard your domestic partner was seen with Jimmy's domestic partner drinking domestic beers in your domestic living space. Is it true? Not very domestic of him. Best keep your domestic partner on a domestic leash. Collar too. Domestic ball and chain. How domestic of my domestic partner, look at him folding my domestic underwear in our domestic home. I'll cook domestic foods for my domestic partner and my domestic partner will domestically do the dishes. Domestically, we are quite happily domestic partnered. Domestic bliss really, domestically speaking. We are regular in our domestic behavior. We've learned many things domestically about each other in our domestic lives. We are domestic every day. Regular and domestic. Domestic the same length of time every day. We are domestic. Quite domestic. Domestically speaking, rather regular in our domestic behavior. Domestic we are every day. Every day domestic. Domestically.

Us Gays Call You Auntie Sylvia

Because any straight woman with man troubles is our best friend.
        Dead or alive. In fact, dead can often be better,
less trouble. Though we know very little of your sorrow.

Most of us will never find a man as hard to love as Ted Hughes,
        nor will most of us care if the man we love fucks
another as long as he tells us all about it in bed, side by side.

Oh Auntie Sylvia, you really were a drama queen. I've learned
        a thing or two about how to hate someone
as beautifully and startlingly as you did.

All the books on you always mention how 1963 was one
        of the coldest winters on record as if you killed
yourself to get warm, which really would put a strange twist

on your biography. I turn thirty this year. The same age you
        were that winter you sealed your children
in a room and stuck your head in the oven.

Ending it all at thirty seems a little scary. A little over the top.
        I've had my own drama. I've shouted in public.
I've tossed an elbow here and there. I've drank too much.

I've acted the fool. I've been jealous and paranoid. The thing
        is, everyone loves to read about insanity,
but few are willing to witness it or put up with it.

Maybe this is our special bond. You lived your own crazy.
        Never apologized. Oh Auntie, I don't really want
to understand you, but let's pretend, for just a bit,

that your troubles are my troubles. Your oven, my oven.

STANDING IN FRONT OF POLLOCK'S
GREYED RAINBOW, CHICAGO, 2012

Three years before you died, Jackson,
  you painted a greyed rainbow,
    which doesn't look anything
like an actual rainbow,
  but you knew that.

There's so much paint here.
  Thick, heavy paint.
    I stand to the side to see it bulging
  off the canvas.
Splotches clotted there like blood or semen.

They call your death "untimely,"
  but, of course, you were driving drunk.
    You'd been falling apart slowly,
then quickly like the changing of seasons.
  "Untimely" seems a little forgiving.
    That's all I'm saying.

Honestly, I get a little hard
  standing here in front
of your canvas, imagining you
  standing over it,
    flicking your paintbrush
with just the right snap of your wrist.

I wonder what it would feel like on skin.
  Like cum erupting from a cock?
Or more gentle like getting pissed on?

Of course, it's 2012, so I imagine you as Ed Harris.
　　　Movies do that to people.
　　　　　　Don't worry, Harris is hot as you.
　　　Plays you well.
And Marcia Gay Harden won an Oscar
　　　　　　for playing Lee,
　　　　　　　　　bad bangs and all.

Here in Chicago, I stand before your *Greyed Rainbow*
　　　and I can almost feel your hands on me,
　　　　　　taking me rough on the gallery floor,
　　　beating me up just a little,
making me your fag
　　　　　　(GLAAD's not going to like that I just said that).

It's March and I forgot how grey it gets
　　　in the Midwest during winter.
　　　　　　How dreary.
　　　　　　I forgot that early March is still winter.
Florida has spoiled me with sunshine
　　　and too many cocktails.
You know what I mean, Jackson?

Three years after you painted this, you crashed
　　　your car, which killed you
　　　　　　and that girl.
Your paintings got more expensive.
　　　Frank O'Hara wrote a poem.
　　　　　　Many poems, really.
　　　Just a step away.
He loved you.
　　　A little like I love you.
But my love is,
　　　of course,
　　　　　　untimely.

Housewife Etiquette: Rule 13

Let him speak first. You may have many things to tell him, but this isn't the time. He's tired. Don't mention complaints or anything unsettling or unpleasant. Fix him his favorite drink. Take him to his favorite chair. Remove his shoes carefully. When you do speak, keep your voice low, soft, and soothing.

SHOOTING CROWS

The crow on the bench beside me
could mean trouble ahead: death,
which I guess is always ahead or above
or below. I read somewhere that not
all crow sightings are bad omens.
Three crows means a wedding, four
a birth, five riches, but by eight
we are back to grief. Nine a secret.
Ten sorrow. I only see the one watching
me. Twitching his head back and forth
as if he might suddenly speak.
What's my bad news, crow? To be honest,
I hate birds. Don't trust them.
There's something prehistoric,
something ancient in the way they move.
They know something I don't,
which is reason enough to fear them.
Some Native Americans call crows the left-handed
guardians of sacred law, which seems
slightly comforting when faced with one,
but I fear you need to be spiritual
for the crow to be your guardian.
He'll see right through me. Already has,
I'm sure. Ted Hughes turned to the crow
after Plath's death. Wrote a whole book
using a crow as a mythical everyman,
as a combination of God, bird, and human.
Something about the great battle
between good and evil, which maybe
gave him comfort, but I doubt it.
In the end, there's no great battle.
Everything falls to the center.

In the United States, it's illegal to film
crows for commercial use. Something
to do with the Migratory Bird Treaty Act.
The HBO series *Six Feet Under* used
a Pied Crow instead of a regular crow
for their opening credits. Had to paint
the bird's chest from white to black.
I guess painting a bird is legal.
Maybe this one here is also hiding
some white, hiding another identity,
not just a plain, old crow. I'd reach out
and check if I wasn't afraid of disease
or losing an eye. One crow. One man.
No film cameras. What's the omen?
When he flies away, like all birds
eventually do, I'll imagine he's off to join
ten of his friends, because someone
once told me that eleven crows means love.

PERRY MASON: *THE CASE OF THE MUTATED CELLS*

One needs evidence to prove a case.
A dead wife in a plane crash. Her name
not on the passengers' list. No marriage
license on record. A dead son with
leukemia. No blood cell counts. No
medical records. No birth certificate.
No one ever saw or spoke to either.
Two phantom bodies. Two beards
to fit your face, Mr. Burr. What would
Perry Mason say? You claimed your
greatest regret in life was accepting
the role that made you famous,
which you played for nine seasons,
plus 26 made-for-TV movies
which aired in the 80s and early 90s:
my childhood. I watched your brooding
masculine face in black and white
and in color. My mother beside me,
always a lover of mysteries, of cases
solved by the show's end. Had I known
you were gay, Mr. Burr, I would've
watched with greater intensity trying
to spot the lover of men in each
of your moves. Your fake dead wife
and son, plus your quickly annulled
"on the record" marriage to Isabella
Ward, and one more unverified
marriage to a woman who conveniently
died three years later, couldn't stop you
from falling in love right there on the CBS
set of *Perry Mason*. You and Robert
bonded over orchids, which is pretty gay,
if I say so myself. You went the long haul

with him: thirty years. Then you died
of cancer yourself. Real cancer.
Documented cancer, like the leukemia
taking hold of my mother right now.
Our phone calls have turned to medical
updates: platelet counts, bone marrow
results, CT scans. She's still the same
mother in the same body, but a body
that has betrayed us all. You know how
that is, Mr. Burr, don't you? Your desires
surfacing among the lies. I need
evidence that she'll make it the longest
possible. I need proof. I need Perry
to fight my mother's case, to condemn
her mutated cells, to lock them up
as tight as a closet door in 1950's
Hollywood. I need to believe
in everything working out by the time
the credits roll and I see your name
and Robert's name glowing together
on the TV screen.

Tonight I Dream of January Jones
in a Supermarket in Florida

This isn't the same as the dream where I meet Betty
in the soup aisle, and she slaps my face, abandons her cart,

and walks off in the opposite direction. Both of us never
speaking a word. No, this is different. Calmer.

January's in the produce gracefully picking tomatoes,
avocados, mangos. Almost like Ginsberg watching

Whitman eyeing the grocery boys, yet she eyes only
the fruits and vegetables, and the boys seem to have

only eyes for me. I stay back, afraid to speak,
remembering her during a late night talk show

saying she doesn't get approached by fans and thinks
it's because she looks mean. I wouldn't say mean,

maybe cold, above the rest. Her blonde hair is shiny
even in the poor lighting of this shitty grocery store

where I can't ever find what I'm looking for.
Even my dream can't make this place elegant

or enchanting or any other e-word you can think of.
The dream is just me staring at her as she fills her cart

with produce. One piece on top of another and then
another and another. It will soon overflow. Her body

unable to stop. Unable to see the mess it's creating:

the sudden breaking open of melon on the floor,

juices filling cracked tile. The handsome grocery boys
are looking now. Annoyed at the pretty woman

oblivious to all the destruction she's leaving in her wake.

A History of the Unmarried

Frank O'Hara loved Vincent in code:
(F) hearts (V). It's hard to love a dancer.
You never know where they're going,
how to bend their bodies, everything
popping and cracking, and then, suddenly,
no dancer in your bed. Is it harder to hold
on to a body with no paperwork? No
signed document? No vow? You dress
in the morning, button your uniform,
lace your boots. You are not a dancer.
You kiss me once and leave for the day.
I stay here in the apartment that has almost
destroyed us. So much sunlight.
I wash the dishes, fold the laundry,
sweep the floor like some mad 1960's
housewife. We are the unmarried.
The undocumented. The unlabeled.
Stein loved Alice. Alice loved Stein's laugh.
Like two voices merging and bellowing
from the same lips that kissed her nipples,
her cheeks, her lips. Stein coded her work:
tender buttons. But she also used the word gay
over a hundred times in one piece,
and she meant our gay. Homosexual gay.
Love between two of the same. But are we
the same? You and I? We are the unmarried.
The undocumented. The unlabeled. Fearing
exile, deportation, excommunication.
I don't code the letters I leave around
the house reminding you to pick up toilet
paper, to take the trash out, to love me.
We don't code our fights. Staring at each
other from across the couch, an actual storm

raging outside. Is this how it ends?
I wonder how hard it would be to remove
you from my life. To drag the pink eraser
across our years, leaving shards of rubber
in its wake. The paper never the same.
But we don't have any paper. We are
the unmarried. The undocumented.
The unlabeled. We are just two men
choosing to stay.

HOUSEWIFE ETIQUETTE: RULE 17

Wear something delicate to bed that will please your husband. Remember you are the mother to his children and not his lady of the night. Be classy and respectful. Soft pink or purple are good colors. If he needs relief, make sure to please him. Don't expect too much. Don't seem overly excited. Make sure to turn off the lights.

Obama Says Same-Sex Couples Should Be Allowed to Marry, May 2012

"I think about members of my own staff
who are in incredibly committed
monogamous relationships, same-sex
relationships, who are raising kids together,"

—President Obama

The man next to me isn't you.
He's taller. Hair shorter. Skin
darker. You're on his other side.
The sheets on the floor. The dog
scratching the door. Everyone
naked. Everyone still. The sudden
peace that comes from release.
We don't know his name.
It doesn't matter. He is a body.
You are a body. I am a body.
Nothing more. Soon, he'll rise
and dress. Legs into pants. Shirt
over head. I'll slide underwear
up thighs. You'll find an old pair
of gym shorts. We'll walk him
to the door. He'll kiss our mouths.
Thank us. It's unlikely we'll see
him again. Tonight, you'll buy
groceries. I'll cook dinner. We'll
sit at my dead grandma's table
and talk of the future. Of a move
North. We'll watch episodes
of *Seinfeld* on DVD and eat cereal
as a late night snack. You'll walk
the dog. I'll load the dishwasher.
Brush my teeth. Slide into sheets

and wait for the heat of your body.
The soft fur of your chest. Your
hands on skin. In bed, you'll slowly
and deliberately make me cum.
I'll kiss your mouth. You'll stroke
the hair on my ass. We'll roll
into each other and sleep will
come. First for you. Always
quick. Then for me. Our bodies
falling into familiar rhythms.

On Turning Thirty

"I am thirty this November.
You are still small, in your fourth year.
We stand watching the yellow leaves go queer,
Flapping in the winter rain,
Falling flat and washed."

—Anne Sexton, "The Double Image"

I, too, am thirty this November.
Thankfully, no little ones to apologize to,
or console, or make up for lost time.
I've made it through three decades
without procreating, which seems a feat
for most. Being two men together helps,
I guess. We are finally back North away
from the land of sand, palm trees, and too
much sunlight. I'd forgotten the smell
of crushed leaves. How refreshing the fall
air can be in lungs deep. How cold the toilet
seat can get and the boards beneath my feet
as I leave you in bed asleep. I'm thirty
today and not feeling nearly as dramatic
as other poets predicted. Perhaps I'll grow
wiser, happier, stronger. I've spent
my twenties falling in love then falling apart.
Coming to terms with adulthood,
disappointment, my own mind.
We've been side by side for nearly a decade.
We've moved from Indiana to Florida
to New York City where we wake today
in the chill of November air. We aren't boys,
but I'm not quite sure if we are men,
or if I will ever be one. I'm leaving a decade
behind. A decade spent in sunshine

where we had our fun, but almost lost our way—
blinded. Here, we stand watching queer
leaves go from yellow to brown. The winter
coming fast. Your fingers icy on the white
of my skin. Too pale for beaches. My cropped
red hair in need of a hat. My body older.
My face still young. I'm turning.
Turning thirty this November day.

STANDING WITH YOU IN FRONT OF POLLOCK'S ONE: NUMBER 31, NEW YORK, 2012

That's a lie.
      You're here somewhere.
Probably in the next gallery,
      or down the steps,
          or in the overpriced café,
but not here with me
      in front of Pollock.

We aren't standing together
      like I imagined we might:
          hand in hand, admiring
      how the splatters of paint
hit the canvas.

It's just me
      and a gaggle of strangers:
tourists with cameras,
      student groups,
          security guards reminding
everyone not to use flash.

But I tune them out and it's just me
      and Pollock. Yes, you, Jackson.
See there,
      I just changed the address
          of the poem.
The "you" getting all mixed up
          like different colors of paint
      falling at random
          from a dripping brush
in a balding man's hand.

Cigarette in mouth.
         Fag, if you are British.

To be honest,
         I can't help but see semen
when I look at your paintings, Jackson.
         Nature is you.
                  In you.
What's more natural than cum?
         The life-giving juice.
I mean this less vulgarly
                  than it sounds.

Here in New York,
         I feel you, Jackson, at every turn,
                  on every sidewalk,
in every cocktail I sip—gulp really.
         You're here in this gallery,
on this wall,
         on this street,
                  in this city,

and so is my man—
         suddenly, behind me,
his hand on my ass,
         or is that your hand, Jackson?
Drunk again,
         and grasping for life,
for another bucket of paint,
                  for someone else's
         nature.

When the Indian Guy Cried During Sex

I wondered if it was at the beauty of our love
on display before him. Our clothes mixing
in the open closet, which he could see
from the bed where I moved inside him,
where you kissed his mouth, where tears
ran down his cheeks. But now I remember
a girl in a poetry workshop a few years ago
telling me never to write "I wonder"
in a poem, but I do wonder about those tears,
which probably had nothing to do with
love, ours or anyone else's. Perhaps
he was actually uncomfortable with my
cock inside him but too shy to say something—
his desire to be a good guest star
easing the pain. Or maybe he's really just
an emotional wreck, crazy, unstable, with his
own problems—problems that, thankfully,
aren't ours to solve. Now I'm wondering
if I should have said he was Indian.
It's just a fact. Like it's a fact that he cried,
that I moved inside him, that you were there,
that afterwards you and I had Indian food
in the city and didn't speak of his tears,
but laughed at each other and wondered
if life would always be like this.

A Drunk Man Tells Me He's a Sex Addict
on the 4th of July

I'm drunk too on the subway heading home
    from a bar where I moved through darkness
in nothing but a jockstrap and harness.

Though we didn't speak, this man was there too.
    Now he wants me to guess his age.
I say mid-forties to please him and it works.

He's really 58, which is the same age as my mother
    whose birthday was just a day ago.
He's proud of his worked-out body, his diet,

his efforts to avoid the inevitable slip of skin over
    bone. It's almost worked.
We're nearly alone on this train heading uptown.

It's the Fourth of July, or it was. The 5th now.
    He questions me: my age, my relationship
status, what I was doing in that bar, if I like it there,

if I engage in the "activities" in the bathroom.
    I tell him I prefer the dark corners by the pool
table. When he hears about you he wants all the details:

how you're out of town, how we've been together
    for nearly a decade, how we love each other,
yet find sexual release in the arms of other men,

how we want to find true happiness. The kind most
    never do. He's never been in a serious
relationship and thinks he's missed out.

Says at first he blamed it on being positive.
        Been positive since the 80s, beating the odds.
That's when he says he's a sex addict.

But I think this is perhaps an excuse too.
        What classifies an addict? How is he any
different than me? I've spent the night with my tongue

in mouths I do not know, my fingers on/in asses
        of strangers, left my cum on a man's thigh
in an elevator that serves as a store: jocks, dildos,

poppers. A sex addict? I don't know. And yes,
        I've seen that Michael Fassbender movie,
but didn't see what the big deal was.

And yes, my therapist called me hypersexual
        in our second session, but he was a fool,
and I eventually gave up on him. On therapy.

The drunk man is rambling now. Repeating himself.
        Tells me again he's positive. This time
he puts his hand up to his mouth as if to hide

the words which he speaks in the same loud volume.
        He tells me he's Jewish and asks if I'm Irish
(my red hair glowing in the subway train's yellow light).

I tell him *yes*, which is mostly a lie. I don't actually know
        much of my own heritage. My grandmother
once told me about a famous Native American

we are all related to, but even a drunk man
        isn't going to think of me as part Native
American, so for him I'll be Irish. Before I get off

the train, he grabs my hand, tells me our talk has left
     him melancholy. Not sad, not depressed.
Melancholy. His eyes are soft, face wrinkled:

things his weightlifting cannot fix. I say, *Perhaps*
     we'll meet again and leave him alone on the train
barreling north to a small apartment where he will strip

off his clothes, look in the mirror, and try to imagine
     two bodies holding each other in the way
that only men who've been together for years can.

WE FELL IN LOVE WHEN THE GAP WAS STILL COOL

and Hugh Grant was making a comeback.
His perfect British grin on the wall of my
dorm room that first night you came to me.
Me in my green Gap T-shirt. The one you
would later take and wear yourself.
The sharing of clothes another symbol
of our unstoppable love like the characters
in a Hugh Grant romantic comedy.
And it was you who took me to see
Love Actually on my twenty-first birthday
in our matching striped Gap sweaters—
almost matching anyway (different colors).
There we sat: two boys laughing, almost
crying, but most definitely holding hands
in my hometown in Indiana where I spent
middle school nights in that very theater,
packed tight with friends, seeing bad movie
after bad movie. It never really mattered.
Like it doesn't matter now holding hands
nearly ten years later in a different theater,
in a different city, far from that dorm room
where we first sat and watched *About a Boy*.
Our hands inching closer and closer
and then finally our lips, followed by
the first removal of a Gap T-shirt, jeans,
underwear. Hugh Grant smiling down
on our young naked bodies.

Questioning if We Should Get Married
While Watching *Rear Window*

Stella says, *Every man is ready for marriage*
when the right girl comes along. How about
the right boy? It's been nine years
of you staring at me from across the space
of a couch or a table or a bed. Marriage
between two men is legal here in the Empire
State. Just 35 dollars for the license.
Men do it all the time. They stand in tuxes.
Take vows. Place rings on "correct" fingers.
On the TV screen, Jeff doesn't want
to marry Lisa in all her grace. Thankfully,
I have very little. He says, *There's an intelligent*
way to approach marriage. Lisa saunters around
his apartment in her expensive dress
(which she will wear only once). She exudes
confidence, class, and sex as only a 1950's
actress can. She is Grace Kelly at her finest.
And he is Jimmy Stewart playing the macho
photographer attempting to push her away.
His leg in a cast. He'd rather watch the neighbors
act out silent movies before his open windows.
Something we can suddenly relate to
having just moved to the city of peeping toms.
A whole race of them as Stella would say.
The sexy man across the alleyway is showering
again. We can see his dark silhouette scrubbing
away the grit of the day, and I wish the glass
wasn't so frosted. I've watched him for six
weeks. Shirtless in the kitchen. Rising from bed.
A glow of light off somewhere. I've created
my own storylines. None of which involve

murder. I prefer the sexier kind: booty calls
at 3 AM, porn shoots, orgies in the morning.
I should call him Mr. Torso, for that's all he is
to me: a figure living a separate, yet not so private,
life. What does he see looking in at us?
My legs propped on your lap. The dog at your feet.
Raymond Burr on the screen trying to cover up
the murder of his fictional wife. Attacking Grace
Kelly in her red heels. Can Mr. Torso see
that I love you more than I'll ever be able to
put into the meal I cook you each night
or the love that we make in bed (blinds down)?
That I fear a life without you? That everything
we've done has led us here to this new
apartment in New York where we watch
old movies and talk of marriage? Or is he
worried we'll murder each other? That one
body will go missing? The blinds never rising?
That I'll pack my bags, place your jewelry
in your favorite man purse, and try to skip town?
Wait, how did I become the murderer?
Harlem doesn't care that we're gay or my arm
links with yours as we walk down the sidewalk.
It's strange for people to care so little.
It's anticlimactic. This talk of marriage.
The real possibility of it. It won't change us,
or complete us, or mold us into something
more normal, more acceptable, more average.
It won't bend our rules. Or alter our lives
parading silently before Mr. Torso. Both of us
admiring the curves of his body in the glass.
Both of us wishing he'd leave the window
open when he showers.

Doubles

Same stop. Same train. Two gay men with cellos. One case black. One silver. They do not know each other. This is New York where two gay men with cellos can be at the exact same place at the exact same time and not know each other. That's the thing about the city: there's always someone out there just like you. Your double. Might read the same books. Buy the same clothes. Play the same instrument. They talk. These two men with cellos because that is what you do when you meet your double. Especially when your double is cute and gay like you. Gay as in the butt-fucking kind. Not the happy kind. Though these two look fairly happy and musically talented too or so I assume from the size of their cellos. That's a bad sexual joke. Cellos are the same size I think. I know very little about music and I haven't taken the time to look up cello sizes. I went to the symphony once as a kid. It was Halloween. All the musicians wore costumes and I couldn't help but stare at the man with the udder sticking straight out of his crotch. Or was it a she? I don't know. It didn't matter at the time. These men of course are not dressed as cows. One is starting his master's today. The other is off to rehearsal. These cellos have brought them together and because of that they will be in love by 42nd Street or maybe 59th by the way the one is moving his arms. His voice rising in excitement. This will be the beginning of something. And they will say *Oh yes, we met on the subway, both carrying cellos, how strange is that?* But it's not that strange. That's what I'm saying. People meet every day in this city where people carry their whole lives in bags on their backs. Yes this is the beginning of something but also the end in a way. The end of mystery. They've discovered a double but what they don't know is how hard the road ahead will be. The road that begins after that first date in a restaurant or a bar where they will both be amazed at all they have in common. They will sit with wide mouths as they discover their shared love of *Mad Men*, Jackson Pollock paintings, and Grace Kelly. This will make them tipsy on the pure magic of it all which will cause them to fall into each other's arms barely making it to the bed where clothes will be removed and sex will be made. For it will not be love. Not that first time. For there will only be one cello in the room: pressed against the wall. Its shadow stretching long and thin over their bodies which over time will slowly pull to each side of the bed discovering that secret spot where one goes back to two.

SOMEONE SOMEWHERE IS GOOGLING "STONEWALL," INAUGURATION DAY, 2013

A screen is filling with black and white images:
police officers, drag queens, and a few actual
stone walls. There are links to history pages,
organizations that have taken the name,
and the website for the bar where it all began.
A bar that now makes its money off of tourists
paying homage to the riots, raising a gin
and tonic to a movement that's still not over,
but has changed direction. Today, people talk
of marriage. Of becoming like everyone else.
It's cold outside and inside our Harlem
apartment. A place that knows something
about fighting, about surviving, about deciding
how to be equal. Here on this day our computer
screen is filled with a president taking a second
term. A president we've fought to keep.
A president willing to acknowledge our fight.
We've learned to adapt, you and I. To find
our own meaning. Our own way into love,
sex, happiness. In the coming years, we'll make
choices, and yes, one day, we'll probably be
legally tied to each other. Protected under
the law. Written down in the history books.
Two men. Two names. Two bodies.
But that act, no matter how simple or elegant,
will never capture our lives, or our history,
or our desire to be undefined.

ECSTASY IN REVERSE

At 30 I'm hovering over a public toilet
      (not yet filthy) taking my first tab
of ecstasy. Like a teenage raver from the 1990s,
      I'm cracking the capsule with my teeth
like the gay dealer in Chelsea suggested.
      I swallow and wait. Nervous.
Of course, I know other stalls are full
      of stronger drugs going into noses
and veins. This is not my first circuit party,
      but my inherited Midwest devotion
to sensationalized news programming has always
      made me drug cautious. I remember
watching *Dateline* as a kid and witnessing
      their undercover investigation
into the dangers of ecstasy, how some teens died
      after taking it just once. Of course,
I didn't know at the time that they were just stupid
      and didn't hydrate. Yes, I've done my research.
Don't get me wrong, I'm no saint, but my high
      has always come from sex and liquor.
I'm old-fashioned that way. Sometimes it feels
      like I'm living in reverse.
Somehow more responsible at 20 than at 30.
      Had more things figured out too.
Now I'm here in New York taking ecstasy
      and working as a part-time English
professor who can barely pay his bills. That's a lie.
      I can't pay my bills. But you are here
reminding me that I'm lucky in love.
      We find each other and move through bodies
to the dance floor in only our jockstraps
      (nothing new there). We wait for the effects

to hit us, for the lights to begin to blur, to stream
        with the thumping bass. It hits me first:
tingles mixed with waves of nausea. I laugh,
        pull your hand away and then back to
my bare skin. Everything feels a little more intense,
        but then I want to throw up in my mouth,
but I don't think I can, and I hate throwing up
        more than anything in this whole world.
I mean that. More than genocide or child prostitution
        or Katy Perry songs. We follow each other
to the bar to buy waters then to the bathroom
        to piss them out. We dance. Kiss.
Explore the sensations rushing through our skin
        like electricity. Later I laugh in your ear
and I say, *I still prefer gin.* We find our way back
        to our clothes and then to the door.
We link arms and walk to the subway station
        that is completely empty because it is 6 AM
on a Sunday. We take the train back uptown,
        and as we exit the station, we pause
to admire the yellow railing burning bright like egg
        yolks against a skillet or a speeding school bus.
On the sidewalk, the streetlights streak together
        in the early dawn creating one long streamer
across the March sky. Your hand is tucked
        into my pocket: pulsing, tingling, and fully alive.

Standing in Front of Lee Krasner's *Untitled*, New York, 2013

Threads so thin
of paint so thick
on a canvas small,
compact, confined.

In 1948, you painted
this as Pollock's wife.
His shadow long
and slim. Rocky

years by his side:
pushing, loving, fighting.
I found a photograph
of you and him on a beach

not being artists,
just being people
in the sand in bathing
suits with tans

and squinting eyes
into the bright sun.
Yes, there were happy days.
Proof is in the photograph.

Your Parents Say *Okay*

Which is better than the letter "k"
tapped into a cell phone and sent
over miles of land to your hand
here in New York. Yes, that would
be worse, if we are looking for
the bright side of things, the silver
lining, which I'm not known to do.
The *okay* was in person, but not
exactly the response "normal" people
expect when they tell their parents
they're getting married. But what
do we know of normal? It was your
mother who stood in the dust of your
Midwest driveway before you left
for college, looked you in the eye,
and asked, *Can't you just be normal?*
I imagine her like a Faulkner character:
tobacco-weathered skin, short dye-
damaged hair, small tight lips barely
getting the words out. *Can't you just
be normal?* It's the *just* like the *okay*
that stings and makes us laugh
because there's nothing left to do
or say. *Okay*, like you said *I'm going
to the store to buy toilet paper* or *I'm starting
a stamp collection* or *I'm learning to kayak.*
Though those might have produced
questions: *Can you also pick up milk?
Why not coins? Isn't kayaking a lot of work?*
But marriage, marriage to your boyfriend
of ten years, marriage to me,
warrants *just* an *okay.*

Slicing Limes for Dustin

"and what does it mean
if he tells his wife she's unpleasant or dull
and what
does
it mean
if his wife takes sleeping pills or walks
in front of a car?"

—Diane Wakoski, *"Slicing Oranges for Jeremiah"*

And what does it mean to stand in a kitchen
slicing limes for cocktails?
Limes for Dustin?
For drinks we will consume
which will make us happy for a time
then horny
angry
sleepy
depressed
and maybe
if we are lucky
fully alive for just a second?

And what does it mean
that we can't eat as many limes as we want?
That we can so easily get sick
on the citrus?
Stomachs aching?
What does it mean to care
for a sick person?
To wash his body?
Comb his hair?
And what does it mean
for a body to show signs of stopping?

Or for a mind to get confused?
To regret an action?
To do the things it never thought possible?

What does it mean
to stand here
taking care
of you
taking care of me?
To find comfort in this knife
puncturing the bright green skin
of a lime?
Green balls of light.

And what does it mean to fall in love again
and again
with limes in drinks
and the cutting board
smeared with pulp?
Or to go out into the city
and dance
with other bodies?
To be on display?
To have more drinks with sliced limes?
Limes cut by other hands
by other men
in other places.

And what does it mean for an old queen to say
we don't live in the real New York?
That it's gone?
Dead?
That somehow only one person's experience
is real?
And what does it mean
to never want to be that old queen?

To never be that jaded?
And what does it mean
that we stood outside
the Stonewall Inn and drank cocktails
with limes
on the day the Supreme Court
struck down DOMA?
Was that not real?
And what does it mean to only look backward?
To always be longing for another decade?
Another time?

And what does it mean for two men
to be protected
under the law?
To call each other husband?
And what does it mean to know
that if we ever want to leave
each other
it will have to be official?
Paperwork goes both ways.

And what does it mean to become
a housewife voluntarily?
To slice limes for a husband?
Limes for Dustin?
And what does it mean to be married
yet remain queer?
Remain two men in love?
Bonded together?
What does it mean?

A
HISTORY
OF THE
UNMARRIED

NOTES

The opening quotation of the book is from Frank O'Hara's poem "Mayakovsky," which was also quoted in the first episode of season two of AMC's *Mad Men*.

The line "yes I said yes I will Yes." is from James Joyce's *Ulysses*.

"A History of Marriage," "Not My Mother," "You Don't Kiss Boys, Boys Kiss You," "Shut up, Betty! You're Drunk," and "Tonight I Dream of January Jones in a Supermarket in Florida" refer to or use lines from AMC's *Mad Men*.

"Housewife Etiquette: Rule 1," "Housewife Etiquette: Rule 9," "Housewife Etiquette: Rule 13," and "Housewife Etiquette: Rule 17" are based on a guide to being a good wife, which was included in 1950's textbooks.

"Counting Bears" is for Dustin, Mark, Josh, Brian, and Richard and is partly inspired by the poems "The 59th Bear" and "Grand Canyon" by Ted Hughes.

"On Becoming Domestic Partners, Orlando, 2012" is a play off of Gertrude Stein's "Miss Furr and Miss Skeene."

ACKNOWLEDGMENTS

I'm grateful to the following journals where some of these poems previously appeared or will soon appear (sometimes in different versions):

The Antioch Review ("Mistaken Identity"); *Chelsea Station* ("Real Men Love Jesus"); *Grist* ("Seeing a Dead Lizard After Reading Mark Doty's 'Turtle, Swan'"); *Velvet Mafia* ("We've Done This All Backwards"); *Wilde Magazine* ("A Stranger Asks: Who's the Man and Who's the Woman?" and "Holding Hands Outside a Pro-Family Rally with my Seed Inside You"); *Berfrois* ("Watching *Sylvia* While You Cart the Dying"); *Referential Magazine* ("Someone Somewhere is Googling 'Stonewall,' Inauguration Day, 2013" and "Not Telling My Parents I'm in Therapy While Driving Over the Sunshine Skyway Bridge, Which Collapsed 31 Years Ago"); *Polari Journal* ("Obama Says Same-Sex Couples Should Be Allowed to Marry, May 2012"); *Hobble Creek Review* ("Tonight I Dream of January Jones in a Supermarket in Florida"); *Assaracus* ("Election Night, November 2008," "Standing in Front of Pollock's *Greyed Rainbow*, Chicago 2012," "Us Gays Call You Auntie Sylvia," "On Turning Thirty," and "When the Indian Guy Cried During Sex"); *SmokeLong Quarterly* ("Doubles"); *Weave* ("Counting Bears" and "A History of the Unmarried); *The Account* ("A History of Marriage" and "Slicing Limes for Dustin"); *The Los Angeles Review* ("On Becoming Domestic Partners, Orlando 2012"); The Cossack Review ("Shooting Crows")

I'm thankful to Valerie Wetlaufer and Jaclyn Sullivan for their eyes, thoughts, and support of this book.

This book wouldn't have happened without the many talented people (living and dead) who inspired me including

Frank O'Hara, Sylvia Plath, Ted Hughes, Anne Sexton, Diane Wakoski, Gertrude Stein, Jackson Pollock, Lee Krasner, Alfred Hitchcock, Raymond Burr, Mark Doty, Matthew Weiner, and January Jones.

I'm forever grateful to Bryan Borland who has not only supported my work for years, but has given me a poetry family.

Lastly, I'm thankful for the support of my family (blood and non-blood) and my husband.

About the Author

Stephen S. Mills is the author of the Lambda Award-winning book *He Do the Gay Man in Different Voices* (Sibling Rivalry Press, 2012). He earned his MFA from Florida State University. His work has appeared in *The Antioch Review, The Gay and Lesbian Review Worldwide, PANK, The New York Quarterly, The Los Angeles Review, Knockout, Assaracus, The Rumpus,* and others. He is also the winner of the 2008 Gival Press Oscar Wilde Poetry Award. He lives in New York City.

www.stephensmills.com

About the Press

Sibling Rivalry Press is an independent publishing house based in Little Rock, Arkansas. Our mission is to publish work that disturbs and enraptures.

www.siblingrivalrypress.com

CPSIA information can be obtained at www.ICGtesting.com
Printed in the USA
LVOW11s0035140115

422542LV00007B/235/P

9 781937 420796